CAMPING JOURNAL

This Book Belongs to

Name :

Phone :

Address :

TRIP # _____

FROM / TO	
ROUTE	
MILEAGE	

WEATHER CONDITIONS

🌡 _____   ☀ ⛅ ☁ 🌧 ❄

🚩 _____   ☐ ☐ ☐ ☐ ☐

DATE

CAMPGROUND

NAME	LOCATION	☆☆☆☆☆
ADDRESS	SHOWERS	☆☆☆☆☆
PHONE	CAMPSTORE	☆☆☆☆☆
WEBSITE	LAUNDRY	☆☆☆☆☆
SITE #	WATER PRESSURE	☆☆☆☆☆
PRICE	OVERALL RATING	☆☆☆☆☆

HIGHLIGHTS

PLACES & ACTIVITIES

DINING & RESTAURANTS

TRIP # ____

- FROM / TO
- ROUTE
- MILEAGE

WEATHER CONDITIONS

- 🌡️ ____ ☀️ ⛅ 🌧️ ⛈️ ❄️
- 🚩 ____ ☐ ☐ ☐ ☐ ☐
- 📅 DATE

CAMPGROUND

NAME	LOCATION	☆☆☆☆☆
ADDRESS	SHOWERS	☆☆☆☆☆
PHONE	CAMPSTORE	☆☆☆☆☆
WEBSITE	LAUNDRY	☆☆☆☆☆
SITE #	WATER PRESSURE	☆☆☆☆☆
PRICE	OVERALL RATING	☆☆☆☆☆

HIGHLIGHTS

PLACES & ACTIVITIES

DINING & RESTAURANTS

TRIP # ____

🗺️ FROM / TO	
🗺️ ROUTE	
🚫 MILEAGE	

WEATHER CONDITIONS

🌡️ ____ ☀️ ⛅ 🌧️ ⛈️ ❄️

🏳️ ____ ☐ ☐ ☐ ☐ ☐

📅 DATE

CAMPGROUND

🏕️ NAME		🏘️ LOCATION	☆☆☆☆☆
📍 ADDRESS		🚿 SHOWERS	☆☆☆☆☆
📞 PHONE		🏬 CAMPSTORE	☆☆☆☆☆
🌐 WEBSITE		👕 LAUNDRY	☆☆☆☆☆
⛺ SITE #		🚰 WATER PRESSURE	☆☆☆☆☆
💵 PRICE		🤲 OVERALL RATING	☆☆☆☆☆

HIGHLIGHTS

PLACES & ACTIVITIES

DINING & RESTAURANTS

TRIP # ____

⌖ FROM / TO	
🗺 ROUTE	
🧭 MILEAGE	

WEATHER CONDITIONS

🌡 ____ ☀️ ⛅ 🌧 ⛈ ❄️

🚩 ____ ☐ ☐ ☐ ☐ ☐

📅 DATE

CAMPGROUND

🏕 NAME		🏙 LOCATION	☆☆☆☆☆
📍 ADDRESS		🚿 SHOWERS	☆☆☆☆☆
📞 PHONE		🏪 CAMPSTORE	☆☆☆☆☆
🌐 WEBSITE		👕 LAUNDRY	☆☆☆☆☆
🏕 SITE #		🚰 WATER PRESSURE	☆☆☆☆☆
💵 PRICE		🤲 OVERALL RATING	☆☆☆☆☆

HIGHLIGHTS

PLACES & ACTIVITIES

DINING & RESTAURANTS

TRIP # _____

📍 FROM / TO	
🗺️ ROUTE	
🔘 MILEAGE	

WEATHER CONDITIONS

🌡️ _____ ☀️ ⛅ 🌧️ ⛈️ ❄️

🚩 _____ ☐ ☐ ☐ ☐ ☐

📅 DATE

CAMPGROUND

🏕️ NAME	🏕️ LOCATION	☆☆☆☆☆
📍 ADDRESS	🚿 SHOWERS	☆☆☆☆☆
📞 PHONE	🏪 CAMPSTORE	☆☆☆☆☆
🌐 WEBSITE	👕 LAUNDRY	☆☆☆☆☆
SITE #	🚰 WATER PRESSURE	☆☆☆☆☆
💵 PRICE	🖐️ OVERALL RATING	☆☆☆☆☆

HIGHLIGHTS

PLACES & ACTIVITIES

DINING & RESTAURANTS

TRIP # ____

- FROM / TO
- ROUTE
- MILEAGE

WEATHER CONDITIONS

☼ ⛅ 🌧 ⛈ ❄

☐ ☐ ☐ ☐ ☐

DATE

CAMPGROUND

NAME	LOCATION	☆☆☆☆☆
ADDRESS	SHOWERS	☆☆☆☆☆
PHONE	CAMPSTORE	☆☆☆☆☆
WEBSITE	LAUNDRY	☆☆☆☆☆
SITE #	WATER PRESSURE	☆☆☆☆☆
PRICE	OVERALL RATING	☆☆☆☆☆

HIGHLIGHTS

PLACES & ACTIVITIES

DINING & RESTAURANTS

TRIP # ____

FROM / TO	
ROUTE	
MILEAGE	

WEATHER CONDITIONS

☼ ⛅ ☁ 🌧 ⛈ ❄

☐ ☐ ☐ ☐ ☐

DATE

CAMPGROUND

NAME		LOCATION	☆☆☆☆☆
ADDRESS		SHOWERS	☆☆☆☆☆
PHONE		CAMPSTORE	☆☆☆☆☆
WEBSITE		LAUNDRY	☆☆☆☆☆
SITE #		WATER PRESSURE	☆☆☆☆☆
PRICE		OVERALL RATING	☆☆☆☆☆

HIGHLIGHTS

PLACES & ACTIVITIES

DINING & RESTAURANTS

TRIP # _____

FROM / TO	
ROUTE	
MILEAGE	

WEATHER CONDITIONS

☀ ⛅ 🌧 ⛈ ❄

☐ ☐ ☐ ☐ ☐

DATE

CAMPGROUND

NAME	LOCATION	☆☆☆☆☆
ADDRESS	SHOWERS	☆☆☆☆☆
PHONE	CAMPSTORE	☆☆☆☆☆
WEBSITE	LAUNDRY	☆☆☆☆☆
SITE #	WATER PRESSURE	☆☆☆☆☆
PRICE	OVERALL RATING	☆☆☆☆☆

HIGHLIGHTS

PLACES & ACTIVITIES

DINING & RESTAURANTS

TRIP # ____

FROM / TO	
ROUTE	
MILEAGE	

WEATHER CONDITIONS

		☀	⛅	🌧	⛈	❄
🌡	___					
🚩	___	☐	☐	☐	☐	☐

DATE

CAMPGROUND

NAME		LOCATION	☆☆☆☆☆
ADDRESS		SHOWERS	☆☆☆☆☆
PHONE		CAMPSTORE	☆☆☆☆☆
WEBSITE		LAUNDRY	☆☆☆☆☆
SITE #		WATER PRESSURE	☆☆☆☆☆
PRICE		OVERALL RATING	☆☆☆☆☆

HIGHLIGHTS

PLACES & ACTIVITIES

DINING & RESTAURANTS

TRIP # _____

FROM / TO	
ROUTE	
MILEAGE	

WEATHER CONDITIONS

☀ ⛅ 🌧 ⛈ ❄

☐ ☐ ☐ ☐ ☐

DATE ___

CAMPGROUND

NAME	LOCATION	☆☆☆☆☆
ADDRESS	SHOWERS	☆☆☆☆☆
PHONE	CAMPSTORE	☆☆☆☆☆
WEBSITE	LAUNDRY	☆☆☆☆☆
SITE #	WATER PRESSURE	☆☆☆☆☆
PRICE	OVERALL RATING	☆☆☆☆☆

HIGHLIGHTS

PLACES & ACTIVITIES

DINING & RESTAURANTS

TRIP # ____

FROM / TO	
ROUTE	
MILEAGE	

WEATHER CONDITIONS

🌡 ____ ☀ ⛅ 🌧 ⛈ ❄

🚩 ____ ☐ ☐ ☐ ☐ ☐

DATE

CAMPGROUND

NAME	LOCATION	☆☆☆☆☆
ADDRESS	SHOWERS	☆☆☆☆☆
PHONE	CAMPSTORE	☆☆☆☆☆
WEBSITE	LAUNDRY	☆☆☆☆☆
SITE #	WATER PRESSURE	☆☆☆☆☆
PRICE	OVERALL RATING	☆☆☆☆☆

HIGHLIGHTS

PLACES & ACTIVITIES

DINING & RESTAURANTS

TRIP # ____

FROM / TO	
ROUTE	
MILEAGE	

WEATHER CONDITIONS

🌡 ____ ☀ ⛅ ☁ 🌧 ❄

🏳 ____ ☐ ☐ ☐ ☐ ☐

📅 DATE

CAMPGROUND

NAME		LOCATION	☆☆☆☆☆
ADDRESS		SHOWERS	☆☆☆☆☆
PHONE		CAMPSTORE	☆☆☆☆☆
WEBSITE		LAUNDRY	☆☆☆☆☆
SITE #		WATER PRESSURE	☆☆☆☆☆
PRICE		OVERALL RATING	☆☆☆☆☆

HIGHLIGHTS

PLACES & ACTIVITIES

DINING & RESTAURANTS

TRIP # _____

FROM / TO	
ROUTE	
MILEAGE	

WEATHER CONDITIONS

Temperature _____ ☀ ⛅ ☁ 🌧 ❄

Wind _____ ☐ ☐ ☐ ☐ ☐

DATE

CAMPGROUND

NAME		LOCATION	☆☆☆☆☆
ADDRESS		SHOWERS	☆☆☆☆☆
PHONE		CAMPSTORE	☆☆☆☆☆
WEBSITE		LAUNDRY	☆☆☆☆☆
SITE #		WATER PRESSURE	☆☆☆☆☆
PRICE		OVERALL RATING	☆☆☆☆☆

HIGHLIGHTS

PLACES & ACTIVITIES

DINING & RESTAURANTS

TRIP # _____

🗺️ FROM / TO	
🗺️ ROUTE	
🧭 MILEAGE	

WEATHER CONDITIONS

🌡️ _____ ☀️ ⛅ 🌧️ ⛈️ ❄️

🚩 _____ ☐ ☐ ☐ ☐ ☐

📅 DATE

CAMPGROUND

🏕️ NAME		🏞️ LOCATION	☆☆☆☆☆
📍 ADDRESS		🚿 SHOWERS	☆☆☆☆☆
📞 PHONE		🏪 CAMPSTORE	☆☆☆☆☆
🌐 WEBSITE		👕 LAUNDRY	☆☆☆☆☆
🏕️ SITE #		🚰 WATER PRESSURE	☆☆☆☆☆
💵 PRICE		🤲 OVERALL RATING	☆☆☆☆☆

HIGHLIGHTS

PLACES & ACTIVITIES

DINING & RESTAURANTS

TRIP # _____

FROM / TO	
ROUTE	
MILEAGE	

WEATHER CONDITIONS

🌡 _____ ☀ ⛅ ☁ 🌧 ❄

🏴 _____ ☐ ☐ ☐ ☐ ☐

DATE

CAMPGROUND

NAME		LOCATION	☆☆☆☆☆
ADDRESS		SHOWERS	☆☆☆☆☆
PHONE		CAMPSTORE	☆☆☆☆☆
WEBSITE		LAUNDRY	☆☆☆☆☆
SITE #		WATER PRESSURE	☆☆☆☆☆
PRICE		OVERALL RATING	☆☆☆☆☆

HIGHLIGHTS

PLACES & ACTIVITIES

DINING & RESTAURANTS

TRIP # ____

FROM / TO	
ROUTE	
MILEAGE	

WEATHER CONDITIONS

☀ ⛅ 🌧 ⛈ ❄

☐ ☐ ☐ ☐ ☐

DATE

CAMPGROUND

NAME		LOCATION	☆☆☆☆☆
ADDRESS		SHOWERS	☆☆☆☆☆
PHONE		CAMPSTORE	☆☆☆☆☆
WEBSITE		LAUNDRY	☆☆☆☆☆
SITE #		WATER PRESSURE	☆☆☆☆☆
PRICE		OVERALL RATING	☆☆☆☆☆

HIGHLIGHTS

PLACES & ACTIVITIES

DINING & RESTAURANTS

TRIP # ____

FROM / TO	
ROUTE	
MILEAGE	

WEATHER CONDITIONS

🌡️ ____ ☀️ ⛅ 🌧️ ⛈️ ❄️

🚩 ____ ☐ ☐ ☐ ☐ ☐

DATE

CAMPGROUND

NAME		LOCATION	☆☆☆☆☆
ADDRESS		SHOWERS	☆☆☆☆☆
PHONE		CAMPSTORE	☆☆☆☆☆
WEBSITE		LAUNDRY	☆☆☆☆☆
SITE #		WATER PRESSURE	☆☆☆☆☆
PRICE		OVERALL RATING	☆☆☆☆☆

HIGHLIGHTS

PLACES & ACTIVITIES

DINING & RESTAURANTS

TRIP # ____

FROM / TO	
ROUTE	
MILEAGE	

WEATHER CONDITIONS

🌡 ____ ☀ 🌤 🌧 ⛈ ❄

🏳 ____ ☐ ☐ ☐ ☐ ☐

DATE

CAMPGROUND

NAME		LOCATION	☆☆☆☆☆
ADDRESS		SHOWERS	☆☆☆☆☆
PHONE		CAMPSTORE	☆☆☆☆☆
WEBSITE		LAUNDRY	☆☆☆☆☆
SITE #		WATER PRESSURE	☆☆☆☆☆
PRICE		OVERALL RATING	☆☆☆☆☆

HIGHLIGHTS

PLACES & ACTIVITIES

DINING & RESTAURANTS

TRIP # _____

FROM / TO

ROUTE

MILEAGE

WEATHER CONDITIONS

_____

_____

DATE

CAMPGROUND

NAME	LOCATION	☆☆☆☆☆
ADDRESS	SHOWERS	☆☆☆☆☆
PHONE	CAMPSTORE	☆☆☆☆☆
WEBSITE	LAUNDRY	☆☆☆☆☆
SITE #	WATER PRESSURE	☆☆☆☆☆
PRICE	OVERALL RATING	☆☆☆☆☆

HIGHLIGHTS

PLACES & ACTIVITIES

DINING & RESTAURANTS

TRIP # _____

FROM / TO	
ROUTE	
MILEAGE	

WEATHER CONDITIONS

🌡️ _____ ☀️ ⛅ 🌧️ ⛈️ ❄️

🎏 _____ ☐ ☐ ☐ ☐ ☐

📅 DATE

CAMPGROUND

NAME		LOCATION	☆☆☆☆☆
ADDRESS		SHOWERS	☆☆☆☆☆
PHONE		CAMPSTORE	☆☆☆☆☆
WEBSITE		LAUNDRY	☆☆☆☆☆
SITE #		WATER PRESSURE	☆☆☆☆☆
PRICE		OVERALL RATING	☆☆☆☆☆

HIGHLIGHTS

PLACES & ACTIVITIES

DINING & RESTAURANTS

TRIP # ____

FROM / TO	
ROUTE	
MILEAGE	

WEATHER CONDITIONS

🌡 ____ ☀ ⛅ 🌧 ⛈ ❄

🚩 ____ ☐ ☐ ☐ ☐ ☐

DATE

CAMPGROUND

NAME		LOCATION	☆☆☆☆☆
ADDRESS		SHOWERS	☆☆☆☆☆
PHONE		CAMPSTORE	☆☆☆☆☆
WEBSITE		LAUNDRY	☆☆☆☆☆
SITE #		WATER PRESSURE	☆☆☆☆☆
PRICE		OVERALL RATING	☆☆☆☆☆

HIGHLIGHTS

PLACES & ACTIVITIES

DINING & RESTAURANTS

TRIP # ____

FROM / TO	
ROUTE	
MILEAGE	

WEATHER CONDITIONS

🌡 ____   ☀ 🌤 🌧 ⛈ ❄

🚩 ____   ☐ ☐ ☐ ☐ ☐

📅 DATE

CAMPGROUND

NAME		LOCATION	☆☆☆☆☆
ADDRESS		SHOWERS	☆☆☆☆☆
PHONE		CAMPSTORE	☆☆☆☆☆
WEBSITE		LAUNDRY	☆☆☆☆☆
SITE #		WATER PRESSURE	☆☆☆☆☆
PRICE		OVERALL RATING	☆☆☆☆☆

HIGHLIGHTS

PLACES & ACTIVITIES

DINING & RESTAURANTS

TRIP # ____

FROM / TO	
ROUTE	
MILEAGE	

WEATHER CONDITIONS

🌡 ____ ☀ ⛅ 🌧 ⛈ ❄

🚩 ____ ☐ ☐ ☐ ☐ ☐

DATE

CAMPGROUND

NAME		LOCATION	☆☆☆☆☆
ADDRESS		SHOWERS	☆☆☆☆☆
PHONE		CAMPSTORE	☆☆☆☆☆
WEBSITE		LAUNDRY	☆☆☆☆☆
SITE #		WATER PRESSURE	☆☆☆☆☆
PRICE		OVERALL RATING	☆☆☆☆☆

HIGHLIGHTS

PLACES & ACTIVITIES

DINING & RESTAURANTS

TRIP # _____

FROM / TO	
ROUTE	
MILEAGE	

WEATHER CONDITIONS

🌡 _____   ☀ ⛅ 🌧 ⛈ ❄
💨 _____   ☐ ☐ ☐ ☐ ☐

📅 DATE

CAMPGROUND

NAME		LOCATION	☆☆☆☆☆
ADDRESS		SHOWERS	☆☆☆☆☆
PHONE		CAMPSTORE	☆☆☆☆☆
WEBSITE		LAUNDRY	☆☆☆☆☆
SITE #		WATER PRESSURE	☆☆☆☆☆
PRICE		OVERALL RATING	☆☆☆☆☆

HIGHLIGHTS

PLACES & ACTIVITIES

DINING & RESTAURANTS

TRIP # _____

FROM / TO	
ROUTE	
MILEAGE	

WEATHER CONDITIONS

🌡 _____ ☀ ⛅ 🌧 ⛈ ❄

🚩 _____ ☐ ☐ ☐ ☐ ☐

DATE

CAMPGROUND

NAME		LOCATION	☆☆☆☆☆
ADDRESS		SHOWERS	☆☆☆☆☆
PHONE		CAMPSTORE	☆☆☆☆☆
WEBSITE		LAUNDRY	☆☆☆☆☆
SITE #		WATER PRESSURE	☆☆☆☆☆
PRICE		OVERALL RATING	☆☆☆☆☆

HIGHLIGHTS

PLACES & ACTIVITIES

DINING & RESTAURANTS

TRIP # _____

FROM / TO

ROUTE

MILEAGE

WEATHER CONDITIONS

_____

_____

DATE

CAMPGROUND

NAME	LOCATION	☆☆☆☆☆
ADDRESS	SHOWERS	☆☆☆☆☆
PHONE	CAMPSTORE	☆☆☆☆☆
WEBSITE	LAUNDRY	☆☆☆☆☆
SITE #	WATER PRESSURE	☆☆☆☆☆
PRICE	OVERALL RATING	☆☆☆☆☆

HIGHLIGHTS

PLACES & ACTIVITIES

DINING & RESTAURANTS

TRIP # _____

- FROM / TO
- ROUTE
- MILEAGE

WEATHER CONDITIONS

🌡 _____ ☀ ⛅ 🌧 ⛈ ❄
🚩 _____ ☐ ☐ ☐ ☐ ☐

📅 DATE

CAMPGROUND

NAME	LOCATION	☆☆☆☆☆
ADDRESS	SHOWERS	☆☆☆☆☆
PHONE	CAMPSTORE	☆☆☆☆☆
WEBSITE	LAUNDRY	☆☆☆☆☆
SITE #	WATER PRESSURE	☆☆☆☆☆
PRICE	OVERALL RATING	☆☆☆☆☆

HIGHLIGHTS

PLACES & ACTIVITIES

DINING & RESTAURANTS

TRIP # _____

FROM / TO	
ROUTE	
MILEAGE	

WEATHER CONDITIONS

🌡 _____ ☀ ⛅ 🌧 ⛈ ❄

🎏 _____ ☐ ☐ ☐ ☐ ☐

📅 DATE

CAMPGROUND

NAME		LOCATION		☆☆☆☆☆
ADDRESS		SHOWERS		☆☆☆☆☆
PHONE		CAMPSTORE		☆☆☆☆☆
WEBSITE		LAUNDRY		☆☆☆☆☆
SITE #		WATER PRESSURE		☆☆☆☆☆
PRICE		OVERALL RATING		☆☆☆☆☆

HIGHLIGHTS

PLACES & ACTIVITIES

DINING & RESTAURANTS

TRIP # _____

FROM / TO	
ROUTE	
MILEAGE	

WEATHER CONDITIONS

🌡️ _____ ☀️ ⛅ 🌧️ ⛈️ ❄️

🚩 _____ ☐ ☐ ☐ ☐ ☐

📅 DATE

CAMPGROUND

NAME		LOCATION	☆☆☆☆☆
ADDRESS		SHOWERS	☆☆☆☆☆
PHONE		CAMPSTORE	☆☆☆☆☆
WEBSITE		LAUNDRY	☆☆☆☆☆
SITE #		WATER PRESSURE	☆☆☆☆☆
PRICE		OVERALL RATING	☆☆☆☆☆

HIGHLIGHTS

PLACES & ACTIVITIES

DINING & RESTAURANTS

TRIP # ____

FROM / TO	
ROUTE	
MILEAGE	

WEATHER CONDITIONS

Temperature: ____   ☀ ⛅ 🌧 ⛈ ❄

Wind: ____   ☐ ☐ ☐ ☐ ☐

DATE

CAMPGROUND

NAME	LOCATION	☆☆☆☆☆
ADDRESS	SHOWERS	☆☆☆☆☆
PHONE	CAMPSTORE	☆☆☆☆☆
WEBSITE	LAUNDRY	☆☆☆☆☆
SITE #	WATER PRESSURE	☆☆☆☆☆
PRICE	OVERALL RATING	☆☆☆☆☆

HIGHLIGHTS

PLACES & ACTIVITIES

DINING & RESTAURANTS

TRIP # _____

- **FROM / TO**
- **ROUTE**
- **MILEAGE**

WEATHER CONDITIONS

🌡 _____   ☀ ⛅ 🌧 ⛈ ❄
🏳 _____   ☐ ☐ ☐ ☐ ☐

- **DATE**

CAMPGROUND

NAME	LOCATION	☆☆☆☆☆
ADDRESS	SHOWERS	☆☆☆☆☆
PHONE	CAMPSTORE	☆☆☆☆☆
WEBSITE	LAUNDRY	☆☆☆☆☆
SITE #	WATER PRESSURE	☆☆☆☆☆
PRICE	OVERALL RATING	☆☆☆☆☆

HIGHLIGHTS

PLACES & ACTIVITIES

DINING & RESTAURANTS

TRIP # ____

FROM / TO	
ROUTE	
MILEAGE	

WEATHER CONDITIONS

🌡 ____ ☀ ⛅ ☁ 🌧 ❄
🚩 ____ ☐ ☐ ☐ ☐ ☐

📅 DATE

CAMPGROUND

NAME		LOCATION	☆☆☆☆☆
ADDRESS		SHOWERS	☆☆☆☆☆
PHONE		CAMPSTORE	☆☆☆☆☆
WEBSITE		LAUNDRY	☆☆☆☆☆
SITE #		WATER PRESSURE	☆☆☆☆☆
PRICE		OVERALL RATING	☆☆☆☆☆

HIGHLIGHTS

PLACES & ACTIVITIES

DINING & RESTAURANTS

TRIP # _____

FROM / TO	
ROUTE	
MILEAGE	

WEATHER CONDITIONS

🌡 _____ ☀ ⛅ 🌧 ⛈ ❄
🚩 _____ ☐ ☐ ☐ ☐ ☐

📅 DATE

CAMPGROUND

NAME		LOCATION	☆☆☆☆☆
ADDRESS		SHOWERS	☆☆☆☆☆
PHONE		CAMPSTORE	☆☆☆☆☆
WEBSITE		LAUNDRY	☆☆☆☆☆
SITE #		WATER PRESSURE	☆☆☆☆☆
PRICE		OVERALL RATING	☆☆☆☆☆

HIGHLIGHTS

PLACES & ACTIVITIES

DINING & RESTAURANTS

TRIP # ____

FROM / TO	
ROUTE	
MILEAGE	

WEATHER CONDITIONS

🌡 ____ ☀ ⛅ 🌧 ⛈ ❄

🚩 ____ ☐ ☐ ☐ ☐ ☐

📅 DATE

CAMPGROUND

NAME		LOCATION	☆☆☆☆☆
ADDRESS		SHOWERS	☆☆☆☆☆
PHONE		CAMPSTORE	☆☆☆☆☆
WEBSITE		LAUNDRY	☆☆☆☆☆
SITE #		WATER PRESSURE	☆☆☆☆☆
PRICE		OVERALL RATING	☆☆☆☆☆

HIGHLIGHTS

PLACES & ACTIVITIES

DINING & RESTAURANTS

TRIP # _____

FROM / TO	
ROUTE	
MILEAGE	

WEATHER CONDITIONS

☀ ⛅ ☁ 🌧 ❄

☐ ☐ ☐ ☐ ☐

DATE

CAMPGROUND

NAME	LOCATION		☆☆☆☆☆
ADDRESS	SHOWERS		☆☆☆☆☆
PHONE	CAMPSTORE		☆☆☆☆☆
WEBSITE	LAUNDRY		☆☆☆☆☆
SITE #	WATER PRESSURE		☆☆☆☆☆
PRICE	OVERALL RATING		☆☆☆☆☆

HIGHLIGHTS

PLACES & ACTIVITIES

DINING & RESTAURANTS

TRIP # _____

FROM / TO	
ROUTE	
MILEAGE	

WEATHER CONDITIONS

🌡 _____ ☀ ⛅ ☁ 🌧 ❄
🏴 _____ ☐ ☐ ☐ ☐ ☐

DATE

CAMPGROUND

NAME		LOCATION	☆☆☆☆☆
ADDRESS		SHOWERS	☆☆☆☆☆
PHONE		CAMPSTORE	☆☆☆☆☆
WEBSITE		LAUNDRY	☆☆☆☆☆
SITE #		WATER PRESSURE	☆☆☆☆☆
PRICE		OVERALL RATING	☆☆☆☆☆

HIGHLIGHTS

PLACES & ACTIVITIES

DINING & RESTAURANTS

TRIP # _____

FROM / TO	
ROUTE	
MILEAGE	

WEATHER CONDITIONS

🌡 _____   ☀ ⛅ 🌧 ⛈ ❄

💨 _____   ☐ ☐ ☐ ☐ ☐

📅 DATE

CAMPGROUND

NAME		LOCATION	☆☆☆☆☆
ADDRESS		SHOWERS	☆☆☆☆☆
PHONE		CAMPSTORE	☆☆☆☆☆
WEBSITE		LAUNDRY	☆☆☆☆☆
SITE #		WATER PRESSURE	☆☆☆☆☆
PRICE		OVERALL RATING	☆☆☆☆☆

HIGHLIGHTS

PLACES & ACTIVITIES

DINING & RESTAURANTS

TRIP # ____

FROM / TO	
ROUTE	
MILEAGE	

WEATHER CONDITIONS

☀️ ⛅ 🌧️ ⛈️ ❄️

☐ ☐ ☐ ☐ ☐

DATE

CAMPGROUND

NAME	LOCATION	☆☆☆☆☆
ADDRESS	SHOWERS	☆☆☆☆☆
PHONE	CAMPSTORE	☆☆☆☆☆
WEBSITE	LAUNDRY	☆☆☆☆☆
SITE #	WATER PRESSURE	☆☆☆☆☆
PRICE	OVERALL RATING	☆☆☆☆☆

HIGHLIGHTS

PLACES & ACTIVITIES

DINING & RESTAURANTS

TRIP # _____

FROM / TO	
ROUTE	
MILEAGE	

WEATHER CONDITIONS

🌡️ _____   ☀️ ⛅ ☁️ 🌧️ ❄️

💨 _____   ☐ ☐ ☐ ☐ ☐

DATE

CAMPGROUND

NAME		LOCATION	☆☆☆☆☆
ADDRESS		SHOWERS	☆☆☆☆☆
PHONE		CAMPSTORE	☆☆☆☆☆
WEBSITE		LAUNDRY	☆☆☆☆☆
SITE #		WATER PRESSURE	☆☆☆☆☆
PRICE		OVERALL RATING	☆☆☆☆☆

HIGHLIGHTS

PLACES & ACTIVITIES

DINING & RESTAURANTS

TRIP # _____

FROM / TO	
ROUTE	
MILEAGE	

WEATHER CONDITIONS

☀ ⛅ ☁ 🌧 ❄

	_____	☐ ☐ ☐ ☐ ☐

DATE

CAMPGROUND

NAME		LOCATION	☆☆☆☆☆
ADDRESS		SHOWERS	☆☆☆☆☆
PHONE		CAMPSTORE	☆☆☆☆☆
WEBSITE		LAUNDRY	☆☆☆☆☆
SITE #		WATER PRESSURE	☆☆☆☆☆
PRICE		OVERALL RATING	☆☆☆☆☆

HIGHLIGHTS

PLACES & ACTIVITIES

DINING & RESTAURANTS

TRIP # _____

FROM / TO	
ROUTE	
MILEAGE	

WEATHER CONDITIONS

🌡 _____ ☀ ⛅ 🌧 ⛈ ❄

🚩 _____ ☐ ☐ ☐ ☐ ☐

📅 DATE

CAMPGROUND

NAME		LOCATION	☆☆☆☆☆
ADDRESS		SHOWERS	☆☆☆☆☆
PHONE		CAMPSTORE	☆☆☆☆☆
WEBSITE		LAUNDRY	☆☆☆☆☆
SITE #		WATER PRESSURE	☆☆☆☆☆
PRICE		OVERALL RATING	☆☆☆☆☆

HIGHLIGHTS

PLACES & ACTIVITIES

DINING & RESTAURANTS

TRIP # _____

FROM / TO
ROUTE
MILEAGE

WEATHER CONDITIONS

Temperature: _____ ☀ ⛅ ☁ 🌧 ❄

Wind: _____ ☐ ☐ ☐ ☐ ☐

DATE

CAMPGROUND

NAME	LOCATION	☆☆☆☆☆
ADDRESS	SHOWERS	☆☆☆☆☆
PHONE	CAMPSTORE	☆☆☆☆☆
WEBSITE	LAUNDRY	☆☆☆☆☆
SITE #	WATER PRESSURE	☆☆☆☆☆
PRICE	OVERALL RATING	☆☆☆☆☆

HIGHLIGHTS

PLACES & ACTIVITIES

DINING & RESTAURANTS

TRIP # ____

FROM / TO	
ROUTE	
MILEAGE	

WEATHER CONDITIONS

🌡 ____ ☀ ⛅ 🌧 ⛈ ❄

🚩 ____ ☐ ☐ ☐ ☐ ☐

DATE

CAMPGROUND

NAME	LOCATION	☆☆☆☆☆
ADDRESS	SHOWERS	☆☆☆☆☆
PHONE	CAMPSTORE	☆☆☆☆☆
WEBSITE	LAUNDRY	☆☆☆☆☆
SITE #	WATER PRESSURE	☆☆☆☆☆
PRICE	OVERALL RATING	☆☆☆☆☆

HIGHLIGHTS

PLACES & ACTIVITIES

DINING & RESTAURANTS

TRIP # _____

FROM / TO

ROUTE

MILEAGE

WEATHER CONDITIONS

☀ ⛅ ☁ 🌧 ❄

☐ ☐ ☐ ☐ ☐

DATE

CAMPGROUND

NAME		LOCATION	☆☆☆☆☆
ADDRESS		SHOWERS	☆☆☆☆☆
PHONE		CAMPSTORE	☆☆☆☆☆
WEBSITE		LAUNDRY	☆☆☆☆☆
SITE #		WATER PRESSURE	☆☆☆☆☆
PRICE		OVERALL RATING	☆☆☆☆☆

HIGHLIGHTS

PLACES & ACTIVITIES

DINING & RESTAURANTS

TRIP # _____

FROM / TO	
ROUTE	
MILEAGE	

WEATHER CONDITIONS

🌡 _____ ☀ ⛅ 🌧 ⛈ ❄
🚩 _____ ☐ ☐ ☐ ☐ ☐

DATE

CAMPGROUND

NAME		LOCATION	☆☆☆☆☆
ADDRESS		SHOWERS	☆☆☆☆☆
PHONE		CAMPSTORE	☆☆☆☆☆
WEBSITE		LAUNDRY	☆☆☆☆☆
SITE #		WATER PRESSURE	☆☆☆☆☆
PRICE		OVERALL RATING	☆☆☆☆☆

HIGHLIGHTS

PLACES & ACTIVITIES

DINING & RESTAURANTS

TRIP # _____

FROM / TO	
ROUTE	
MILEAGE	

WEATHER CONDITIONS

🌡 _____ ☀ ⛅ 🌧 ⛈ ❄

🚩 _____ ☐ ☐ ☐ ☐ ☐

📅 DATE

CAMPGROUND

NAME		LOCATION	☆☆☆☆☆
ADDRESS		SHOWERS	☆☆☆☆☆
PHONE		CAMPSTORE	☆☆☆☆☆
WEBSITE		LAUNDRY	☆☆☆☆☆
SITE #		WATER PRESSURE	☆☆☆☆☆
PRICE		OVERALL RATING	☆☆☆☆☆

HIGHLIGHTS

PLACES & ACTIVITIES

DINING & RESTAURANTS

TRIP # _____

FROM / TO	
ROUTE	
MILEAGE	

WEATHER CONDITIONS

🌡 _____ ☀ ⛅ 🌧 ⛈ ❄

💨 _____ ☐ ☐ ☐ ☐ ☐

DATE

CAMPGROUND

NAME		LOCATION	☆☆☆☆☆
ADDRESS		SHOWERS	☆☆☆☆☆
PHONE		CAMPSTORE	☆☆☆☆☆
WEBSITE		LAUNDRY	☆☆☆☆☆
SITE #		WATER PRESSURE	☆☆☆☆☆
PRICE		OVERALL RATING	☆☆☆☆☆

HIGHLIGHTS

PLACES & ACTIVITIES

DINING & RESTAURANTS

TRIP # ____

FROM / TO	
ROUTE	
MILEAGE	

WEATHER CONDITIONS

☀ ⛅ ☁ 🌧 ❄

☐ ☐ ☐ ☐ ☐

DATE

CAMPGROUND

NAME		LOCATION	☆☆☆☆☆
ADDRESS		SHOWERS	☆☆☆☆☆
PHONE		CAMPSTORE	☆☆☆☆☆
WEBSITE		LAUNDRY	☆☆☆☆☆
SITE #		WATER PRESSURE	☆☆☆☆☆
PRICE		OVERALL RATING	☆☆☆☆☆

HIGHLIGHTS

PLACES & ACTIVITIES

DINING & RESTAURANTS

TRIP # _____

- FROM / TO
- ROUTE
- MILEAGE

WEATHER CONDITIONS

🌡 _____ ☀ ⛅ 🌧 ⛈ ❄
🚩 _____ ☐ ☐ ☐ ☐ ☐

📅 DATE

CAMPGROUND

NAME	LOCATION	☆☆☆☆☆
ADDRESS	SHOWERS	☆☆☆☆☆
PHONE	CAMPSTORE	☆☆☆☆☆
WEBSITE	LAUNDRY	☆☆☆☆☆
SITE #	WATER PRESSURE	☆☆☆☆☆
PRICE	OVERALL RATING	☆☆☆☆☆

HIGHLIGHTS

PLACES & ACTIVITIES

DINING & RESTAURANTS

TRIP # _____

FROM / TO

ROUTE

MILEAGE

WEATHER CONDITIONS

🌡 _____ ☀ ⛅ ☁ 🌧 ❄

🚩 _____ ☐ ☐ ☐ ☐ ☐

DATE

CAMPGROUND

NAME		LOCATION	☆☆☆☆☆
ADDRESS		SHOWERS	☆☆☆☆☆
PHONE		CAMPSTORE	☆☆☆☆☆
WEBSITE		LAUNDRY	☆☆☆☆☆
SITE #		WATER PRESSURE	☆☆☆☆☆
PRICE		OVERALL RATING	☆☆☆☆☆

HIGHLIGHTS

PLACES & ACTIVITIES

DINING & RESTAURANTS

TRIP # ____

FROM / TO

ROUTE

MILEAGE

WEATHER CONDITIONS

🌡 ____   ☀ ⛅ 🌧 ⛈ ❄

🌬 ____   ☐ ☐ ☐ ☐ ☐

DATE

CAMPGROUND

NAME		LOCATION	☆☆☆☆☆
ADDRESS		SHOWERS	☆☆☆☆☆
PHONE		CAMPSTORE	☆☆☆☆☆
WEBSITE		LAUNDRY	☆☆☆☆☆
SITE #		WATER PRESSURE	☆☆☆☆☆
PRICE		OVERALL RATING	☆☆☆☆☆

HIGHLIGHTS

PLACES & ACTIVITIES

DINING & RESTAURANTS

TRIP # ____

FROM / TO

ROUTE

MILEAGE

WEATHER CONDITIONS

🌡️ ____   ☀️ ⛅ ☁️ 🌧️ ❄️

🚩 ____   ☐ ☐ ☐ ☐ ☐

DATE

CAMPGROUND

NAME		LOCATION	☆☆☆☆☆
ADDRESS		SHOWERS	☆☆☆☆☆
PHONE		CAMPSTORE	☆☆☆☆☆
WEBSITE		LAUNDRY	☆☆☆☆☆
SITE #		WATER PRESSURE	☆☆☆☆☆
PRICE		OVERALL RATING	☆☆☆☆☆

HIGHLIGHTS

PLACES & ACTIVITIES

DINING & RESTAURANTS

TRIP # _____

FROM / TO	
ROUTE	
MILEAGE	

WEATHER CONDITIONS

☀ ⛅ 🌧 ⛈ ❄

🌡 _____ ☐ ☐ ☐ ☐ ☐

🗖 DATE

CAMPGROUND

NAME		LOCATION	☆☆☆☆☆
ADDRESS		SHOWERS	☆☆☆☆☆
PHONE		CAMPSTORE	☆☆☆☆☆
WEBSITE		LAUNDRY	☆☆☆☆☆
SITE #		WATER PRESSURE	☆☆☆☆☆
PRICE		OVERALL RATING	☆☆☆☆☆

HIGHLIGHTS

PLACES & ACTIVITIES

DINING & RESTAURANTS

TRIP # ____

🗺 FROM / TO	
🗺 ROUTE	
⊘ MILEAGE	

WEATHER CONDITIONS

🌡 ____ ☀ ⛅ ☁ 🌧 ❄

🎏 ____ ☐ ☐ ☐ ☐ ☐

📅 DATE

CAMPGROUND

🏕 NAME	🏕 LOCATION	☆☆☆☆☆
⊙ ADDRESS	🚿 SHOWERS	☆☆☆☆☆
📞 PHONE	🏬 CAMPSTORE	☆☆☆☆☆
🌐 WEBSITE	👕 LAUNDRY	☆☆☆☆☆
⛺ SITE #	🚰 WATER PRESSURE	☆☆☆☆☆
💵 PRICE	🤲 OVERALL RATING	☆☆☆☆☆

HIGHLIGHTS

PLACES & ACTIVITIES

DINING & RESTAURANTS

TRIP # ____

FROM / TO	
ROUTE	
MILEAGE	

WEATHER CONDITIONS

🌡 ____ ☀ ⛅ 🌧 ⛈ ❄

💨 ____ ☐ ☐ ☐ ☐ ☐

📅 DATE

CAMPGROUND

NAME	LOCATION	☆☆☆☆☆
ADDRESS	SHOWERS	☆☆☆☆☆
PHONE	CAMPSTORE	☆☆☆☆☆
WEBSITE	LAUNDRY	☆☆☆☆☆
SITE #	WATER PRESSURE	☆☆☆☆☆
PRICE	OVERALL RATING	☆☆☆☆☆

HIGHLIGHTS

PLACES & ACTIVITIES

DINING & RESTAURANTS

TRIP # _____

🗺 FROM / TO	
📖 ROUTE	
🧭 MILEAGE	

WEATHER CONDITIONS

🌡 _____ ☀️ ⛅ 🌧 ⛈ ❄️

🎏 _____ ☐ ☐ ☐ ☐ ☐

📅 DATE

CAMPGROUND

🏕 NAME		🏞 LOCATION	☆☆☆☆☆
📍 ADDRESS		🚿 SHOWERS	☆☆☆☆☆
📞 PHONE		🏪 CAMPSTORE	☆☆☆☆☆
🌐 WEBSITE		👕 LAUNDRY	☆☆☆☆☆
⛺ SITE #		💧 WATER PRESSURE	☆☆☆☆☆
💵 PRICE		🤲 OVERALL RATING	☆☆☆☆☆

HIGHLIGHTS

PLACES & ACTIVITIES

DINING & RESTAURANTS

TRIP # _____

- 🗺️ FROM / TO
- 🗺️ ROUTE
- 🧭 MILEAGE

WEATHER CONDITIONS

🌡️ _____ ☀️ ⛅ 🌧️ ⛈️ ❄️

🚩 _____ ☐ ☐ ☐ ☐ ☐

📅 DATE

CAMPGROUND

🏕️ NAME	🏞️ LOCATION	☆☆☆☆☆
📍 ADDRESS	🚿 SHOWERS	☆☆☆☆☆
📞 PHONE	🏪 CAMPSTORE	☆☆☆☆☆
🌐 WEBSITE	👕 LAUNDRY	☆☆☆☆☆
🏕️ SITE #	🚰 WATER PRESSURE	☆☆☆☆☆
💰 PRICE	🤲 OVERALL RATING	☆☆☆☆☆

HIGHLIGHTS

PLACES & ACTIVITIES

DINING & RESTAURANTS

TRIP # _____

FROM / TO	
ROUTE	
MILEAGE	

WEATHER CONDITIONS

🌡️ _____ ☀️ ⛅ 🌧️ ⛈️ ❄️

🚩 _____ ☐ ☐ ☐ ☐ ☐

DATE

CAMPGROUND

NAME		LOCATION	☆☆☆☆☆
ADDRESS		SHOWERS	☆☆☆☆☆
PHONE		CAMPSTORE	☆☆☆☆☆
WEBSITE		LAUNDRY	☆☆☆☆☆
SITE #		WATER PRESSURE	☆☆☆☆☆
PRICE		OVERALL RATING	☆☆☆☆☆

HIGHLIGHTS

PLACES & ACTIVITIES

DINING & RESTAURANTS

TRIP # _____

🗺️ FROM / TO

🗺️ ROUTE

🧭 MILEAGE

WEATHER CONDITIONS

🌡️ _____ ☀️ ⛅ 🌧️ ⛈️ ❄️

🌬️ _____ ☐ ☐ ☐ ☐ ☐

📅 DATE

CAMPGROUND

🏕️ NAME	🏞️ LOCATION	☆☆☆☆☆
📍 ADDRESS	🚿 SHOWERS	☆☆☆☆☆
📞 PHONE	🏪 CAMPSTORE	☆☆☆☆☆
🌐 WEBSITE	👕 LAUNDRY	☆☆☆☆☆
🌳 SITE #	🚰 WATER PRESSURE	☆☆☆☆☆
💵 PRICE	✋ OVERALL RATING	☆☆☆☆☆

HIGHLIGHTS

PLACES & ACTIVITIES

DINING & RESTAURANTS

TRIP # _____

FROM / TO

ROUTE

MILEAGE

WEATHER CONDITIONS

🌡 _____ ☀ ⛅ ☁ 🌧 ❄

🏳 _____ ☐ ☐ ☐ ☐ ☐

DATE

CAMPGROUND

NAME	**LOCATION**	☆☆☆☆☆
ADDRESS	**SHOWERS**	☆☆☆☆☆
PHONE	**CAMPSTORE**	☆☆☆☆☆
WEBSITE	**LAUNDRY**	☆☆☆☆☆
SITE #	**WATER PRESSURE**	☆☆☆☆☆
PRICE	**OVERALL RATING**	☆☆☆☆☆

HIGHLIGHTS

PLACES & ACTIVITIES

DINING & RESTAURANTS

TRIP # ____

- FROM / TO
- ROUTE
- MILEAGE

WEATHER CONDITIONS

Temperature ____

Wind ____

- DATE

CAMPGROUND

NAME	LOCATION	☆☆☆☆☆
ADDRESS	SHOWERS	☆☆☆☆☆
PHONE	CAMPSTORE	☆☆☆☆☆
WEBSITE	LAUNDRY	☆☆☆☆☆
SITE #	WATER PRESSURE	☆☆☆☆☆
PRICE	OVERALL RATING	☆☆☆☆☆

HIGHLIGHTS

PLACES & ACTIVITIES

DINING & RESTAURANTS

TRIP # _____

FROM / TO	
ROUTE	
MILEAGE	

WEATHER CONDITIONS

🌡 _____ ☀ ⛅ ☁ 🌧 ❄

🌬 _____ ☐ ☐ ☐ ☐ ☐

📅 DATE

CAMPGROUND

NAME	LOCATION	☆☆☆☆☆
ADDRESS	SHOWERS	☆☆☆☆☆
PHONE	CAMPSTORE	☆☆☆☆☆
WEBSITE	LAUNDRY	☆☆☆☆☆
SITE #	WATER PRESSURE	☆☆☆☆☆
PRICE	OVERALL RATING	☆☆☆☆☆

HIGHLIGHTS

PLACES & ACTIVITIES

DINING & RESTAURANTS

TRIP # ____

- FROM / TO
- ROUTE
- MILEAGE

WEATHER CONDITIONS

🌡 ____   ☀️ ⛅ 🌧 ⛈ ❄️

🌬 ____   ☐ ☐ ☐ ☐ ☐

📅 DATE

CAMPGROUND

NAME	LOCATION	☆☆☆☆☆
ADDRESS	SHOWERS	☆☆☆☆☆
PHONE	CAMPSTORE	☆☆☆☆☆
WEBSITE	LAUNDRY	☆☆☆☆☆
SITE #	WATER PRESSURE	☆☆☆☆☆
PRICE	OVERALL RATING	☆☆☆☆☆

HIGHLIGHTS

PLACES & ACTIVITIES

DINING & RESTAURANTS

TRIP # _____

FROM / TO	
ROUTE	
MILEAGE	

WEATHER CONDITIONS

🌡 _____ ☀ ⛅ ☁ 🌧 ❄

🚩 _____ ☐ ☐ ☐ ☐ ☐

DATE

CAMPGROUND

NAME		LOCATION		☆☆☆☆☆
ADDRESS		SHOWERS		☆☆☆☆☆
PHONE		CAMPSTORE		☆☆☆☆☆
WEBSITE		LAUNDRY		☆☆☆☆☆
SITE #		WATER PRESSURE		☆☆☆☆☆
PRICE		OVERALL RATING		☆☆☆☆☆

HIGHLIGHTS

PLACES & ACTIVITIES

DINING & RESTAURANTS

TRIP # _____

FROM / TO	
ROUTE	
MILEAGE	

WEATHER CONDITIONS

☀ ⛅ 🌧 ⛈ ❄

🌡 _____   ☐ ☐ ☐ ☐ ☐

DATE

CAMPGROUND

NAME		LOCATION	☆☆☆☆☆
ADDRESS		SHOWERS	☆☆☆☆☆
PHONE		CAMPSTORE	☆☆☆☆☆
WEBSITE		LAUNDRY	☆☆☆☆☆
SITE #		WATER PRESSURE	☆☆☆☆☆
PRICE		OVERALL RATING	☆☆☆☆☆

HIGHLIGHTS

PLACES & ACTIVITIES

DINING & RESTAURANTS

TRIP # ____

- **FROM / TO**
- **ROUTE**
- **MILEAGE**

WEATHER CONDITIONS

🌡 ____ ☀ ⛅ ☁ 🌧 ❄

🚩 ____ ☐ ☐ ☐ ☐ ☐

📅 **DATE**

CAMPGROUND

NAME	**LOCATION**	☆☆☆☆☆
ADDRESS	**SHOWERS**	☆☆☆☆☆
PHONE	**CAMPSTORE**	☆☆☆☆☆
WEBSITE	**LAUNDRY**	☆☆☆☆☆
SITE #	**WATER PRESSURE**	☆☆☆☆☆
PRICE	**OVERALL RATING**	☆☆☆☆☆

HIGHLIGHTS

PLACES & ACTIVITIES

DINING & RESTAURANTS

TRIP # ____

FROM / TO	
ROUTE	
MILEAGE	

WEATHER CONDITIONS

	____	☀	⛅	🌧	⛈	❄
	____	☐	☐	☐	☐	☐

DATE

CAMPGROUND

NAME		LOCATION	☆☆☆☆☆
ADDRESS		SHOWERS	☆☆☆☆☆
PHONE		CAMPSTORE	☆☆☆☆☆
WEBSITE		LAUNDRY	☆☆☆☆☆
SITE #		WATER PRESSURE	☆☆☆☆☆
PRICE		OVERALL RATING	☆☆☆☆☆

HIGHLIGHTS

PLACES & ACTIVITIES

DINING & RESTAURANTS

TRIP # _____

FROM / TO

ROUTE

MILEAGE

WEATHER CONDITIONS

☀ 🌤 ☁ 🌧 ❄

☐ ☐ ☐ ☐ ☐

DATE

CAMPGROUND

NAME	LOCATION		☆☆☆☆☆
ADDRESS	SHOWERS		☆☆☆☆☆
PHONE	CAMPSTORE		☆☆☆☆☆
WEBSITE	LAUNDRY		☆☆☆☆☆
SITE #	WATER PRESSURE		☆☆☆☆☆
PRICE	OVERALL RATING		☆☆☆☆☆

HIGHLIGHTS

PLACES & ACTIVITIES

DINING & RESTAURANTS

TRIP # _____

FROM / TO	
ROUTE	
MILEAGE	

WEATHER CONDITIONS

🌡 _____ ☀ ⛅ 🌧 ⛈ ❄

💨 _____ ☐ ☐ ☐ ☐ ☐

📅 DATE

CAMPGROUND

NAME		LOCATION	☆☆☆☆☆
ADDRESS		SHOWERS	☆☆☆☆☆
PHONE		CAMPSTORE	☆☆☆☆☆
WEBSITE		LAUNDRY	☆☆☆☆☆
SITE #		WATER PRESSURE	☆☆☆☆☆
PRICE		OVERALL RATING	☆☆☆☆☆

HIGHLIGHTS

PLACES & ACTIVITIES

DINING & RESTAURANTS

TRIP # ____

FROM / TO

ROUTE

MILEAGE

WEATHER CONDITIONS

🌡 ____ ☀ ⛅ ☁ 🌧 ❄

🚩 ____ ☐ ☐ ☐ ☐ ☐

DATE

CAMPGROUND

NAME		LOCATION	☆☆☆☆☆
ADDRESS		SHOWERS	☆☆☆☆☆
PHONE		CAMPSTORE	☆☆☆☆☆
WEBSITE		LAUNDRY	☆☆☆☆☆
SITE #		WATER PRESSURE	☆☆☆☆☆
PRICE		OVERALL RATING	☆☆☆☆☆

HIGHLIGHTS

PLACES & ACTIVITIES

DINING & RESTAURANTS

TRIP # _____

FROM / TO	
ROUTE	
MILEAGE	

WEATHER CONDITIONS

☀ 🌤 🌧 ⛈ ❄

☐ ☐ ☐ ☐ ☐

DATE

CAMPGROUND

NAME	LOCATION	☆☆☆☆☆
ADDRESS	SHOWERS	☆☆☆☆☆
PHONE	CAMPSTORE	☆☆☆☆☆
WEBSITE	LAUNDRY	☆☆☆☆☆
SITE #	WATER PRESSURE	☆☆☆☆☆
PRICE	OVERALL RATING	☆☆☆☆☆

HIGHLIGHTS

PLACES & ACTIVITIES

DINING & RESTAURANTS

TRIP # _____

FROM / TO	
ROUTE	
MILEAGE	

WEATHER CONDITIONS

🌡 _____   ☀ ⛅ ☁ 🌧 ❄

🚩 _____   ☐ ☐ ☐ ☐ ☐

📅 DATE

CAMPGROUND

NAME		LOCATION	☆☆☆☆☆
ADDRESS		SHOWERS	☆☆☆☆☆
PHONE		CAMPSTORE	☆☆☆☆☆
WEBSITE		LAUNDRY	☆☆☆☆☆
SITE #		WATER PRESSURE	☆☆☆☆☆
PRICE		OVERALL RATING	☆☆☆☆☆

HIGHLIGHTS

PLACES & ACTIVITIES

DINING & RESTAURANTS

TRIP # ____

FROM / TO

ROUTE

MILEAGE

WEATHER CONDITIONS

🌡 ____ ☀ ⛅ ☁ 🌧 ❄

🚩 ____ ☐ ☐ ☐ ☐ ☐

DATE

CAMPGROUND

NAME		LOCATION	☆☆☆☆☆
ADDRESS		SHOWERS	☆☆☆☆☆
PHONE		CAMPSTORE	☆☆☆☆☆
WEBSITE		LAUNDRY	☆☆☆☆☆
SITE #		WATER PRESSURE	☆☆☆☆☆
PRICE		OVERALL RATING	☆☆☆☆☆

HIGHLIGHTS

PLACES & ACTIVITIES

DINING & RESTAURANTS

TRIP # ____

FROM / TO	
ROUTE	
MILEAGE	

WEATHER CONDITIONS

🌡 ____ ☀ ⛅ ☁ 🌧 ❄

🚩 ____ ☐ ☐ ☐ ☐ ☐

📅 DATE

CAMPGROUND

NAME		LOCATION	☆☆☆☆☆
ADDRESS		SHOWERS	☆☆☆☆☆
PHONE		CAMPSTORE	☆☆☆☆☆
WEBSITE		LAUNDRY	☆☆☆☆☆
SITE #		WATER PRESSURE	☆☆☆☆☆
PRICE		OVERALL RATING	☆☆☆☆☆

HIGHLIGHTS

PLACES & ACTIVITIES

DINING & RESTAURANTS

TRIP # ____

- FROM / TO
- ROUTE
- MILEAGE

WEATHER CONDITIONS

- ____ ☀ ⛅ 🌧 ⛈ ❄
- ____ ☐ ☐ ☐ ☐ ☐
- DATE

CAMPGROUND

NAME	LOCATION	☆☆☆☆☆
ADDRESS	SHOWERS	☆☆☆☆☆
PHONE	CAMPSTORE	☆☆☆☆☆
WEBSITE	LAUNDRY	☆☆☆☆☆
SITE #	WATER PRESSURE	☆☆☆☆☆
PRICE	OVERALL RATING	☆☆☆☆☆

HIGHLIGHTS

PLACES & ACTIVITIES

DINING & RESTAURANTS

TRIP # _____

FROM / TO	
ROUTE	
MILEAGE	

WEATHER CONDITIONS

☀ ⛅ ☁ 🌧 ❄
☐ ☐ ☐ ☐ ☐

DATE

CAMPGROUND

NAME		LOCATION	☆☆☆☆☆
ADDRESS		SHOWERS	☆☆☆☆☆
PHONE		CAMPSTORE	☆☆☆☆☆
WEBSITE		LAUNDRY	☆☆☆☆☆
SITE #		WATER PRESSURE	☆☆☆☆☆
PRICE		OVERALL RATING	☆☆☆☆☆

HIGHLIGHTS

PLACES & ACTIVITIES

DINING & RESTAURANTS

TRIP # _____

- FROM / TO
- ROUTE
- MILEAGE

WEATHER CONDITIONS

- _____ ☀ ⛅ ☁ 🌧 ❄
- _____ ☐ ☐ ☐ ☐ ☐
- DATE

CAMPGROUND

NAME	LOCATION	☆☆☆☆☆
ADDRESS	SHOWERS	☆☆☆☆☆
PHONE	CAMPSTORE	☆☆☆☆☆
WEBSITE	LAUNDRY	☆☆☆☆☆
SITE #	WATER PRESSURE	☆☆☆☆☆
PRICE	OVERALL RATING	☆☆☆☆☆

HIGHLIGHTS

PLACES & ACTIVITIES

DINING & RESTAURANTS

TRIP # ____

FROM / TO	
ROUTE	
MILEAGE	

WEATHER CONDITIONS

🌡 ____ ☀ ⛅ 🌧 ⛈ ❄

🚩 ____ ☐ ☐ ☐ ☐ ☐

DATE

CAMPGROUND

NAME		LOCATION	☆☆☆☆☆
ADDRESS		SHOWERS	☆☆☆☆☆
PHONE		CAMPSTORE	☆☆☆☆☆
WEBSITE		LAUNDRY	☆☆☆☆☆
SITE #		WATER PRESSURE	☆☆☆☆☆
PRICE		OVERALL RATING	☆☆☆☆☆

HIGHLIGHTS

PLACES & ACTIVITIES

DINING & RESTAURANTS

TRIP # ____

FROM / TO	
ROUTE	
MILEAGE	

WEATHER CONDITIONS

☀ ⛅ 🌧 ⛈ ❄

☐ ☐ ☐ ☐ ☐

DATE

CAMPGROUND

NAME		LOCATION	☆☆☆☆☆
ADDRESS		SHOWERS	☆☆☆☆☆
PHONE		CAMPSTORE	☆☆☆☆☆
WEBSITE		LAUNDRY	☆☆☆☆☆
SITE #		WATER PRESSURE	☆☆☆☆☆
PRICE		OVERALL RATING	☆☆☆☆☆

HIGHLIGHTS

PLACES & ACTIVITIES

DINING & RESTAURANTS

TRIP # _____

FROM / TO	
ROUTE	
MILEAGE	

WEATHER CONDITIONS

☀️ ⛅ ☁️ 🌧️ ❄️
☐ ☐ ☐ ☐ ☐

DATE

CAMPGROUND

NAME		LOCATION	☆☆☆☆☆
ADDRESS		SHOWERS	☆☆☆☆☆
PHONE		CAMPSTORE	☆☆☆☆☆
WEBSITE		LAUNDRY	☆☆☆☆☆
SITE #		WATER PRESSURE	☆☆☆☆☆
PRICE		OVERALL RATING	☆☆☆☆☆

HIGHLIGHTS

PLACES & ACTIVITIES

DINING & RESTAURANTS

TRIP # ____

- FROM / TO
- ROUTE
- MILEAGE

WEATHER CONDITIONS

☀ ⛅ 🌧 ⛈ ❄
☐ ☐ ☐ ☐ ☐

- DATE

CAMPGROUND

NAME	LOCATION	☆☆☆☆☆
ADDRESS	SHOWERS	☆☆☆☆☆
PHONE	CAMPSTORE	☆☆☆☆☆
WEBSITE	LAUNDRY	☆☆☆☆☆
SITE #	WATER PRESSURE	☆☆☆☆☆
PRICE	OVERALL RATING	☆☆☆☆☆

HIGHLIGHTS

PLACES & ACTIVITIES

DINING & RESTAURANTS

TRIP # ____

FROM / TO	
ROUTE	
MILEAGE	

WEATHER CONDITIONS

☼ ⛅ ☁ 🌧 ❄

☐ ☐ ☐ ☐ ☐

DATE

CAMPGROUND

NAME		LOCATION	☆☆☆☆☆
ADDRESS		SHOWERS	☆☆☆☆☆
PHONE		CAMPSTORE	☆☆☆☆☆
WEBSITE		LAUNDRY	☆☆☆☆☆
SITE #		WATER PRESSURE	☆☆☆☆☆
PRICE		OVERALL RATING	☆☆☆☆☆

HIGHLIGHTS

PLACES & ACTIVITIES

DINING & RESTAURANTS

TRIP # _____

🗺️ FROM / TO

🗺️ ROUTE

⊘ MILEAGE

WEATHER CONDITIONS

🌡️ _____ ☀️ ⛅ 🌧️ ⛈️ ❄️

🚩 _____ ☐ ☐ ☐ ☐ ☐

📅 DATE

CAMPGROUND

🏕️ NAME	🏞️ LOCATION	☆☆☆☆☆
📍 ADDRESS	🚿 SHOWERS	☆☆☆☆☆
📞 PHONE	🏪 CAMPSTORE	☆☆☆☆☆
🌐 WEBSITE	🧺 LAUNDRY	☆☆☆☆☆
🏕️ SITE #	🚰 WATER PRESSURE	☆☆☆☆☆
💵 PRICE	🤲 OVERALL RATING	☆☆☆☆☆

HIGHLIGHTS

PLACES & ACTIVITIES

DINING & RESTAURANTS

TRIP # ____

FROM / TO	
ROUTE	
MILEAGE	

WEATHER CONDITIONS

☀ ⛅ ☁ 🌧 ❄
☐ ☐ ☐ ☐ ☐

DATE

CAMPGROUND

NAME		LOCATION	☆☆☆☆☆
ADDRESS		SHOWERS	☆☆☆☆☆
PHONE		CAMPSTORE	☆☆☆☆☆
WEBSITE		LAUNDRY	☆☆☆☆☆
SITE #		WATER PRESSURE	☆☆☆☆☆
PRICE		OVERALL RATING	☆☆☆☆☆

HIGHLIGHTS

PLACES & ACTIVITIES

DINING & RESTAURANTS

TRIP # _____

- FROM / TO
- ROUTE
- MILEAGE

WEATHER CONDITIONS

☀ ⛅ ☁ 🌧 ❄

☐ ☐ ☐ ☐ ☐

DATE

CAMPGROUND

NAME	LOCATION	☆☆☆☆☆
ADDRESS	SHOWERS	☆☆☆☆☆
PHONE	CAMPSTORE	☆☆☆☆☆
WEBSITE	LAUNDRY	☆☆☆☆☆
SITE #	WATER PRESSURE	☆☆☆☆☆
PRICE	OVERALL RATING	☆☆☆☆☆

HIGHLIGHTS

PLACES & ACTIVITIES

DINING & RESTAURANTS

TRIP # _____

FROM / TO

ROUTE

MILEAGE

WEATHER CONDITIONS

DATE

CAMPGROUND

NAME	LOCATION	☆☆☆☆☆
ADDRESS	SHOWERS	☆☆☆☆☆
PHONE	CAMPSTORE	☆☆☆☆☆
WEBSITE	LAUNDRY	☆☆☆☆☆
SITE #	WATER PRESSURE	☆☆☆☆☆
PRICE	OVERALL RATING	☆☆☆☆☆

HIGHLIGHTS

PLACES & ACTIVITIES

DINING & RESTAURANTS

TRIP # ____

FROM / TO

ROUTE

MILEAGE

WEATHER CONDITIONS

🌡 ____ ☀ ⛅ 🌧 ⛈ ❄

🏳 ____ ☐ ☐ ☐ ☐ ☐

DATE

CAMPGROUND

NAME		LOCATION	☆☆☆☆☆
ADDRESS		SHOWERS	☆☆☆☆☆
PHONE		CAMPSTORE	☆☆☆☆☆
WEBSITE		LAUNDRY	☆☆☆☆☆
SITE #		WATER PRESSURE	☆☆☆☆☆
PRICE		OVERALL RATING	☆☆☆☆☆

HIGHLIGHTS

PLACES & ACTIVITIES

DINING & RESTAURANTS

TRIP # ____

FROM / TO

ROUTE

MILEAGE

WEATHER CONDITIONS

🌡 ____ ☀️ ⛅ ☁️ 🌧 ❄️

🌬 ____ ☐ ☐ ☐ ☐ ☐

DATE

CAMPGROUND

NAME		LOCATION	☆☆☆☆☆
ADDRESS		SHOWERS	☆☆☆☆☆
PHONE		CAMPSTORE	☆☆☆☆☆
WEBSITE		LAUNDRY	☆☆☆☆☆
SITE #		WATER PRESSURE	☆☆☆☆☆
PRICE		OVERALL RATING	☆☆☆☆☆

HIGHLIGHTS

PLACES & ACTIVITIES

DINING & RESTAURANTS

TRIP # ____

FROM / TO	
ROUTE	
MILEAGE	

WEATHER CONDITIONS

🌡 ____ ☀ 🌤 🌧 ⛈ ❄

💨 ____ ☐ ☐ ☐ ☐ ☐

📅 DATE

CAMPGROUND

NAME		LOCATION	☆☆☆☆☆
ADDRESS		SHOWERS	☆☆☆☆☆
PHONE		CAMPSTORE	☆☆☆☆☆
WEBSITE		LAUNDRY	☆☆☆☆☆
SITE #		WATER PRESSURE	☆☆☆☆☆
PRICE		OVERALL RATING	☆☆☆☆☆

HIGHLIGHTS

PLACES & ACTIVITIES

DINING & RESTAURANTS

TRIP # ____

FROM / TO	
ROUTE	
MILEAGE	

WEATHER CONDITIONS

🌡 ____ ☀️ ⛅ ☁️ 🌧 ❄️

🎏 ____ ☐ ☐ ☐ ☐ ☐

DATE

CAMPGROUND

NAME	**LOCATION**	☆☆☆☆☆
ADDRESS	**SHOWERS**	☆☆☆☆☆
PHONE	**CAMPSTORE**	☆☆☆☆☆
WEBSITE	**LAUNDRY**	☆☆☆☆☆
SITE #	**WATER PRESSURE**	☆☆☆☆☆
PRICE	**OVERALL RATING**	☆☆☆☆☆

HIGHLIGHTS

PLACES & ACTIVITIES

DINING & RESTAURANTS

TRIP # ____

📍 FROM / TO	
🗺️ ROUTE	
🧭 MILEAGE	

WEATHER CONDITIONS

🌡️ ____ ☀️ ⛅ 🌧️ ⛈️ ❄️

🚩 ____ ☐ ☐ ☐ ☐ ☐

📅 DATE

CAMPGROUND

🏕️ NAME		🏞️ LOCATION	☆☆☆☆☆
📍 ADDRESS		🚿 SHOWERS	☆☆☆☆☆
📞 PHONE		🏪 CAMPSTORE	☆☆☆☆☆
🌐 WEBSITE		👕 LAUNDRY	☆☆☆☆☆
⛺ SITE #		🚰 WATER PRESSURE	☆☆☆☆☆
💵 PRICE		🤲 OVERALL RATING	☆☆☆☆☆

HIGHLIGHTS

PLACES & ACTIVITIES

DINING & RESTAURANTS

TRIP # _____

FROM / TO

ROUTE

MILEAGE

WEATHER CONDITIONS

_____

_____

DATE

CAMPGROUND

NAME	**LOCATION**	☆☆☆☆☆
ADDRESS	**SHOWERS**	☆☆☆☆☆
PHONE	**CAMPSTORE**	☆☆☆☆☆
WEBSITE	**LAUNDRY**	☆☆☆☆☆
SITE #	**WATER PRESSURE**	☆☆☆☆☆
PRICE	**OVERALL RATING**	☆☆☆☆☆

HIGHLIGHTS

PLACES & ACTIVITIES

DINING & RESTAURANTS

TRIP # ____

- FROM / TO
- ROUTE
- MILEAGE

WEATHER CONDITIONS

DATE

CAMPGROUND

NAME	LOCATION	☆☆☆☆☆
ADDRESS	SHOWERS	☆☆☆☆☆
PHONE	CAMPSTORE	☆☆☆☆☆
WEBSITE	LAUNDRY	☆☆☆☆☆
SITE #	WATER PRESSURE	☆☆☆☆☆
PRICE	OVERALL RATING	☆☆☆☆☆

HIGHLIGHTS

PLACES & ACTIVITIES

DINING & RESTAURANTS

TRIP # _____

FROM / TO	
ROUTE	
MILEAGE	

WEATHER CONDITIONS

☀ ⛅ 🌧 ⛈ ❄
☐ ☐ ☐ ☐ ☐

DATE

CAMPGROUND

NAME		LOCATION	☆☆☆☆☆
ADDRESS		SHOWERS	☆☆☆☆☆
PHONE		CAMPSTORE	☆☆☆☆☆
WEBSITE		LAUNDRY	☆☆☆☆☆
SITE #		WATER PRESSURE	☆☆☆☆☆
PRICE		OVERALL RATING	☆☆☆☆☆

HIGHLIGHTS

PLACES & ACTIVITIES

DINING & RESTAURANTS

TRIP # _____

FROM / TO	
ROUTE	
MILEAGE	

WEATHER CONDITIONS

	☀ ⛅ 🌧 ⛈ ❄
🌡 _____	☐ ☐ ☐ ☐ ☐
DATE	

CAMPGROUND

NAME		LOCATION	☆☆☆☆☆
ADDRESS		SHOWERS	☆☆☆☆☆
PHONE		CAMPSTORE	☆☆☆☆☆
WEBSITE		LAUNDRY	☆☆☆☆☆
SITE #		WATER PRESSURE	☆☆☆☆☆
PRICE		OVERALL RATING	☆☆☆☆☆

HIGHLIGHTS

PLACES & ACTIVITIES

DINING & RESTAURANTS

TRIP # _____

FROM / TO	
ROUTE	
MILEAGE	

WEATHER CONDITIONS

🌡 _____ ☀ ⛅ ☁ 🌧 ❄

💨 _____ ☐ ☐ ☐ ☐ ☐

📅 DATE

CAMPGROUND

NAME		LOCATION	☆☆☆☆☆
ADDRESS		SHOWERS	☆☆☆☆☆
PHONE		CAMPSTORE	☆☆☆☆☆
WEBSITE		LAUNDRY	☆☆☆☆☆
SITE #		WATER PRESSURE	☆☆☆☆☆
PRICE		OVERALL RATING	☆☆☆☆☆

HIGHLIGHTS

PLACES & ACTIVITIES

DINING & RESTAURANTS

TRIP # ____

- **FROM / TO**
- **ROUTE**
- **MILEAGE**

WEATHER CONDITIONS

- 🌡️ ____
- 🚩 ____ ☐ ☐ ☐ ☐ ☐
- **DATE**

CAMPGROUND

NAME	**LOCATION**	☆☆☆☆☆
ADDRESS	**SHOWERS**	☆☆☆☆☆
PHONE	**CAMPSTORE**	☆☆☆☆☆
WEBSITE	**LAUNDRY**	☆☆☆☆☆
SITE #	**WATER PRESSURE**	☆☆☆☆☆
PRICE	**OVERALL RATING**	☆☆☆☆☆

HIGHLIGHTS

PLACES & ACTIVITIES

DINING & RESTAURANTS

TRIP # ____

FROM / TO	
ROUTE	
MILEAGE	

WEATHER CONDITIONS

🌡 ____   ☀ ⛅ 🌧 ⛈ ❄

🎐 ____   ☐ ☐ ☐ ☐ ☐

DATE

CAMPGROUND

NAME		LOCATION	☆☆☆☆☆
ADDRESS		SHOWERS	☆☆☆☆☆
PHONE		CAMPSTORE	☆☆☆☆☆
WEBSITE		LAUNDRY	☆☆☆☆☆
SITE #		WATER PRESSURE	☆☆☆☆☆
PRICE		OVERALL RATING	☆☆☆☆☆

HIGHLIGHTS

PLACES & ACTIVITIES

DINING & RESTAURANTS

TRIP # _____

FROM / TO	
ROUTE	
MILEAGE	

WEATHER CONDITIONS

☀ ⛅ ☁ 🌧 ❄

☐ ☐ ☐ ☐ ☐

DATE

CAMPGROUND

NAME	**LOCATION**	☆☆☆☆☆
ADDRESS	**SHOWERS**	☆☆☆☆☆
PHONE	**CAMPSTORE**	☆☆☆☆☆
WEBSITE	**LAUNDRY**	☆☆☆☆☆
SITE #	**WATER PRESSURE**	☆☆☆☆☆
PRICE	**OVERALL RATING**	☆☆☆☆☆

HIGHLIGHTS

PLACES & ACTIVITIES

DINING & RESTAURANTS

TRIP # _____

🗺 FROM / TO	
🗺 ROUTE	
🚫 MILEAGE	

WEATHER CONDITIONS

🌡 _____ ☀ ⛅ ☁ 🌧 ❄

🏴 _____ ☐ ☐ ☐ ☐ ☐

📅 DATE

CAMPGROUND

🏕 NAME		🏞 LOCATION	☆☆☆☆☆
📍 ADDRESS		🚿 SHOWERS	☆☆☆☆☆
📞 PHONE		🏪 CAMPSTORE	☆☆☆☆☆
🌐 WEBSITE		👕 LAUNDRY	☆☆☆☆☆
🏕 SITE #		🚰 WATER PRESSURE	☆☆☆☆☆
💵 PRICE		🤲 OVERALL RATING	☆☆☆☆☆

HIGHLIGHTS

PLACES & ACTIVITIES

DINING & RESTAURANTS

TRIP # ____

- FROM / TO
- ROUTE
- MILEAGE

WEATHER CONDITIONS

☀ ⛅ 🌧 ⛈ ❄
☐ ☐ ☐ ☐ ☐

DATE

CAMPGROUND

NAME	LOCATION	☆☆☆☆☆
ADDRESS	SHOWERS	☆☆☆☆☆
PHONE	CAMPSTORE	☆☆☆☆☆
WEBSITE	LAUNDRY	☆☆☆☆☆
SITE #	WATER PRESSURE	☆☆☆☆☆
PRICE	OVERALL RATING	☆☆☆☆☆

HIGHLIGHTS

PLACES & ACTIVITIES

DINING & RESTAURANTS

TRIP # ____

FROM / TO

ROUTE

MILEAGE

WEATHER CONDITIONS

☀ ⛅ ☁ 🌧 ❄

▢ ▢ ▢ ▢ ▢

DATE

CAMPGROUND

NAME	LOCATION	☆☆☆☆☆
ADDRESS	SHOWERS	☆☆☆☆☆
PHONE	CAMPSTORE	☆☆☆☆☆
WEBSITE	LAUNDRY	☆☆☆☆☆
SITE #	WATER PRESSURE	☆☆☆☆☆
PRICE	OVERALL RATING	☆☆☆☆☆

HIGHLIGHTS

PLACES & ACTIVITIES

DINING & RESTAURANTS

TRIP # _____

FROM / TO	
ROUTE	
MILEAGE	

WEATHER CONDITIONS

☀ ⛅ ☁ 🌧 ❄

☐ ☐ ☐ ☐ ☐

DATE

CAMPGROUND

NAME		LOCATION	☆☆☆☆☆
ADDRESS		SHOWERS	☆☆☆☆☆
PHONE		CAMPSTORE	☆☆☆☆☆
WEBSITE		LAUNDRY	☆☆☆☆☆
SITE #		WATER PRESSURE	☆☆☆☆☆
PRICE		OVERALL RATING	☆☆☆☆☆

HIGHLIGHTS

PLACES & ACTIVITIES

DINING & RESTAURANTS

TRIP # ____

FROM / TO	
ROUTE	
MILEAGE	

WEATHER CONDITIONS

☀ ⛅ ☁ 🌧 ❄

☐ ☐ ☐ ☐ ☐

DATE

CAMPGROUND

NAME		LOCATION	☆☆☆☆☆
ADDRESS		SHOWERS	☆☆☆☆☆
PHONE		CAMPSTORE	☆☆☆☆☆
WEBSITE		LAUNDRY	☆☆☆☆☆
SITE #		WATER PRESSURE	☆☆☆☆☆
PRICE		OVERALL RATING	☆☆☆☆☆

HIGHLIGHTS

PLACES & ACTIVITIES

DINING & RESTAURANTS

TRIP # ____

FROM / TO	
ROUTE	
MILEAGE	

WEATHER CONDITIONS

🌡 ____ ☀ ⛅ 🌧 ⛈ ❄

💨 ____ ☐ ☐ ☐ ☐ ☐

DATE

CAMPGROUND

NAME	LOCATION	☆☆☆☆☆
ADDRESS	SHOWERS	☆☆☆☆☆
PHONE	CAMPSTORE	☆☆☆☆☆
WEBSITE	LAUNDRY	☆☆☆☆☆
SITE #	WATER PRESSURE	☆☆☆☆☆
PRICE	OVERALL RATING	☆☆☆☆☆

HIGHLIGHTS

PLACES & ACTIVITIES

DINING & RESTAURANTS

TRIP # _____

FROM / TO	
ROUTE	
MILEAGE	

WEATHER CONDITIONS

☀ ⛅ ☁ 🌧 ❄

☐ ☐ ☐ ☐ ☐

DATE

CAMPGROUND

NAME	LOCATION	☆☆☆☆☆
ADDRESS	SHOWERS	☆☆☆☆☆
PHONE	CAMPSTORE	☆☆☆☆☆
WEBSITE	LAUNDRY	☆☆☆☆☆
SITE #	WATER PRESSURE	☆☆☆☆☆
PRICE	OVERALL RATING	☆☆☆☆☆

HIGHLIGHTS

PLACES & ACTIVITIES

DINING & RESTAURANTS

TRIP # _____

FROM / TO	
ROUTE	
MILEAGE	

WEATHER CONDITIONS

🌡 _____ ☀ ⛅ 🌥 🌧 ❄

🏳 _____ ☐ ☐ ☐ ☐ ☐

DATE

CAMPGROUND

NAME		LOCATION	☆☆☆☆☆
ADDRESS		SHOWERS	☆☆☆☆☆
PHONE		CAMPSTORE	☆☆☆☆☆
WEBSITE		LAUNDRY	☆☆☆☆☆
SITE #		WATER PRESSURE	☆☆☆☆☆
PRICE		OVERALL RATING	☆☆☆☆☆

HIGHLIGHTS

PLACES & ACTIVITIES

DINING & RESTAURANTS

TRIP # ____

🧭 FROM / TO	
🗺️ ROUTE	
🚫 MILEAGE	

WEATHER CONDITIONS

🌡️ ____ ☀️ ⛅ 🌥️ 🌧️ ❄️

🚩 ____ ☐ ☐ ☐ ☐ ☐

📅 DATE

CAMPGROUND

🏕️ NAME		🏞️ LOCATION	☆☆☆☆☆
📍 ADDRESS		🚿 SHOWERS	☆☆☆☆☆
📞 PHONE		🏪 CAMPSTORE	☆☆☆☆☆
🌐 WEBSITE		👕 LAUNDRY	☆☆☆☆☆
⛺ SITE #		🚰 WATER PRESSURE	☆☆☆☆☆
💵 PRICE		⭐ OVERALL RATING	☆☆☆☆☆

HIGHLIGHTS

PLACES & ACTIVITIES

DINING & RESTAURANTS

TRIP # _____

🗺 FROM / TO	
🗺 ROUTE	
Ⓝ MILEAGE	

WEATHER CONDITIONS

🌡 _____ ☀ ⛅ 🌧 ⛈ ❄

🚩 _____ ☐ ☐ ☐ ☐ ☐

📅 DATE

CAMPGROUND

🏕 NAME		🏞 LOCATION	☆☆☆☆☆
📍 ADDRESS		🚿 SHOWERS	☆☆☆☆☆
📞 PHONE		🏬 CAMPSTORE	☆☆☆☆☆
🌐 WEBSITE		👕 LAUNDRY	☆☆☆☆☆
🏕 SITE #		🚰 WATER PRESSURE	☆☆☆☆☆
💵 PRICE		✋ OVERALL RATING	☆☆☆☆☆

HIGHLIGHTS

PLACES & ACTIVITIES

DINING & RESTAURANTS

TRIP # _____

🔄 FROM / TO	
🗺️ ROUTE	
⊘ MILEAGE	

WEATHER CONDITIONS

🌡️ _____ ☀️ ⛅ 🌧️ ⛈️ ❄️

🎏 _____ ☐ ☐ ☐ ☐ ☐

📅 DATE

CAMPGROUND

🏕️ NAME		🏞️ LOCATION	☆☆☆☆☆
📍 ADDRESS		🚿 SHOWERS	☆☆☆☆☆
📞 PHONE		🏪 CAMPSTORE	☆☆☆☆☆
🌐 WEBSITE		👕 LAUNDRY	☆☆☆☆☆
🏕️ SITE #		🚰 WATER PRESSURE	☆☆☆☆☆
💵 PRICE		🤲 OVERALL RATING	☆☆☆☆☆

HIGHLIGHTS

PLACES & ACTIVITIES

DINING & RESTAURANTS

TRIP # _____

FROM / TO	
ROUTE	
MILEAGE	

WEATHER CONDITIONS

🌡 _____ ☀ ⛅ ☁ 🌧 ❄

🚩 _____ ☐ ☐ ☐ ☐ ☐

DATE

CAMPGROUND

NAME		LOCATION	☆☆☆☆☆
ADDRESS		SHOWERS	☆☆☆☆☆
PHONE		CAMPSTORE	☆☆☆☆☆
WEBSITE		LAUNDRY	☆☆☆☆☆
SITE #		WATER PRESSURE	☆☆☆☆☆
PRICE		OVERALL RATING	☆☆☆☆☆

HIGHLIGHTS

PLACES & ACTIVITIES

DINING & RESTAURANTS

TRIP # ____

FROM / TO	
ROUTE	
MILEAGE	

WEATHER CONDITIONS

🌡️ ____   ☀️ ⛅ ☁️🌧️ ⛈️ ❄️

🪭 ____   ☐ ☐ ☐ ☐ ☐

📅 DATE

CAMPGROUND

NAME	LOCATION	☆☆☆☆☆
ADDRESS	SHOWERS	☆☆☆☆☆
PHONE	CAMPSTORE	☆☆☆☆☆
WEBSITE	LAUNDRY	☆☆☆☆☆
SITE #	WATER PRESSURE	☆☆☆☆☆
PRICE	OVERALL RATING	☆☆☆☆☆

HIGHLIGHTS

PLACES & ACTIVITIES

DINING & RESTAURANTS

TRIP # _____

FROM / TO	
ROUTE	
MILEAGE	

WEATHER CONDITIONS

☀ ⛅ 🌧 ⛈ ❄
☐ ☐ ☐ ☐ ☐

DATE

CAMPGROUND

NAME	LOCATION	☆☆☆☆☆
ADDRESS	SHOWERS	☆☆☆☆☆
PHONE	CAMPSTORE	☆☆☆☆☆
WEBSITE	LAUNDRY	☆☆☆☆☆
SITE #	WATER PRESSURE	☆☆☆☆☆
PRICE	OVERALL RATING	☆☆☆☆☆

HIGHLIGHTS

PLACES & ACTIVITIES

DINING & RESTAURANTS

TRIP # _____

FROM / TO	
ROUTE	
MILEAGE	

WEATHER CONDITIONS

☀ ⛅ ☁ 🌧 ❄
☐ ☐ ☐ ☐ ☐

DATE

CAMPGROUND

NAME		LOCATION	☆☆☆☆☆
ADDRESS		SHOWERS	☆☆☆☆☆
PHONE		CAMPSTORE	☆☆☆☆☆
WEBSITE		LAUNDRY	☆☆☆☆☆
SITE #		WATER PRESSURE	☆☆☆☆☆
PRICE		OVERALL RATING	☆☆☆☆☆

HIGHLIGHTS

PLACES & ACTIVITIES

DINING & RESTAURANTS

TRIP # ____

- 🗺️ FROM / TO
- 🗺️ ROUTE
- ⭕ MILEAGE

WEATHER CONDITIONS

🌡️ ____ ☀️ ⛅ 🌧️ ⛈️ ❄️

🎐 ____ ☐ ☐ ☐ ☐ ☐

📅 DATE

CAMPGROUND

🏕️ NAME	🏙️ LOCATION	☆☆☆☆☆
📍 ADDRESS	🚿 SHOWERS	☆☆☆☆☆
📞 PHONE	🏪 CAMPSTORE	☆☆☆☆☆
🌐 WEBSITE	👕 LAUNDRY	☆☆☆☆☆
🏕️ SITE #	🚰 WATER PRESSURE	☆☆☆☆☆
💵 PRICE	🤲 OVERALL RATING	☆☆☆☆☆

HIGHLIGHTS

PLACES & ACTIVITIES

DINING & RESTAURANTS

TRIP # _____

FROM / TO	
ROUTE	
MILEAGE	

WEATHER CONDITIONS

🌡 _____ ☀ ⛅ ☁ 🌧 ❄

🎐 _____ ☐ ☐ ☐ ☐ ☐

📅 DATE

CAMPGROUND

NAME		LOCATION	☆☆☆☆☆
ADDRESS		SHOWERS	☆☆☆☆☆
PHONE		CAMPSTORE	☆☆☆☆☆
WEBSITE		LAUNDRY	☆☆☆☆☆
SITE #		WATER PRESSURE	☆☆☆☆☆
PRICE		OVERALL RATING	☆☆☆☆☆

HIGHLIGHTS

PLACES & ACTIVITIES

DINING & RESTAURANTS

TRIP # ____

- FROM / TO
- ROUTE
- MILEAGE

WEATHER CONDITIONS

- DATE

CAMPGROUND

NAME	LOCATION ☆☆☆☆☆
ADDRESS	SHOWERS ☆☆☆☆☆
PHONE	CAMPSTORE ☆☆☆☆☆
WEBSITE	LAUNDRY ☆☆☆☆☆
SITE #	WATER PRESSURE ☆☆☆☆☆
PRICE	OVERALL RATING ☆☆☆☆☆

HIGHLIGHTS

PLACES & ACTIVITIES

DINING & RESTAURANTS

TRIP # _____

FROM / TO	
ROUTE	
MILEAGE	

WEATHER CONDITIONS

🌡️ _____ ☀️ ⛅ 🌧️ 🌧️ ❄️

🚩 _____ ☐ ☐ ☐ ☐ ☐

📅 DATE

CAMPGROUND

NAME		LOCATION	☆☆☆☆☆
ADDRESS		SHOWERS	☆☆☆☆☆
PHONE		CAMPSTORE	☆☆☆☆☆
WEBSITE		LAUNDRY	☆☆☆☆☆
SITE #		WATER PRESSURE	☆☆☆☆☆
PRICE		OVERALL RATING	☆☆☆☆☆

HIGHLIGHTS

PLACES & ACTIVITIES

DINING & RESTAURANTS

TRIP # ____

FROM / TO	
ROUTE	
MILEAGE	

WEATHER CONDITIONS

🌡 ____   ☀ ⛅ 🌧 ⛈ ❄

🚩 ____   ☐ ☐ ☐ ☐ ☐

DATE

CAMPGROUND

NAME	LOCATION	☆☆☆☆☆
ADDRESS	SHOWERS	☆☆☆☆☆
PHONE	CAMPSTORE	☆☆☆☆☆
WEBSITE	LAUNDRY	☆☆☆☆☆
SITE #	WATER PRESSURE	☆☆☆☆☆
PRICE	OVERALL RATING	☆☆☆☆☆

HIGHLIGHTS

PLACES & ACTIVITIES

DINING & RESTAURANTS

Printed in Great Britain
by Amazon